Camouflage

Kamini Khanduri

Contents

	Introduction	3
1	Camouflage	4
2	Animal Homes	6
3	Winter and Summer	8
4	In the Grass	10
5	In the Water	12
6	A New Color	14
7	Is It a Leaf?	16
8	What Is It?	18
	Activities	20
	Projects	36
	Picture Dictionary	38
	About *Read and Discover*	40

OXFORD
UNIVERSITY PRESS

Great Clarendon Street, Oxford, OX2 6DP, United Kingdom

Oxford University Press is a department of the University of Oxford. It furthers the University's objective of excellence in research, scholarship, and education by publishing worldwide. Oxford is a registered trade mark of Oxford University Press in the UK and in certain other countries

© Oxford University Press 2013

The moral rights of the author have been asserted

First published in 2013
2018
10 9 8

No unauthorized photocopying

All rights reserved. No part of this publication may be reproduced, stored in a retrieval system, or transmitted, in any form or by any means, without the prior permission in writing of Oxford University Press, or as expressly permitted by law, by licence or under terms agreed with the appropriate reprographics rights organization. Enquiries concerning reproduction outside the scope of the above should be sent to the ELT Rights Department, Oxford University Press, at the address above

You must not circulate this work in any other form and you must impose this same condition on any acquirer

Links to third party websites are provided by Oxford in good faith and for information only. Oxford disclaims any responsibility for the materials contained in any third party website referenced in this work

ISBN: 978 0 19 464684 0

An Audio Pack containing this book and an Audio download is also available. ISBN 978 0 19 402153 1

This book is also available as an e-Book.
ISBN 978 0 19 410854 6

An accompanying Activity Book is also available.
ISBN 978 0 19 464674 1

Printed in China

This book is printed on paper from certified and well-managed sources.

ACKNOWLEDGEMENTS

Illustrations by: Kelly Kennedy pp.11, 13; Alan Rowe pp.20, 22, 24, 26, 28, 30, 32, 35, 38, 39.

The Publishers would also like to thank the following for their kind permission to reproduce photographs and other copyright material: Alamy pp.4 (Louise Murray), 5 (white spider/Blickwinkel), 16 (katydid/Derrick Alderman); Ardea pp.9 (summer grouse/Tom+Pat Leeson), 12 (flounder/Gavin Parsons), 14 (brown cuttlefish/Gavin Parsons), 17 (leaf gecko/Thomas Marent); Corbis pp.3 (bird/Staffan Widstrand), 5 (bird/Staffan Widstrand), 7 (seals/Michio Hoshino/Minden Pictures), 14 (colourful cuttlefish/Steve Parish/Steve Parish Publishing); Getty Images pp.3 (fish/Reinhard Dirscherl/Waterframe, lion/Beverly Joubert/National Geographic), 7 (monkey/Connie Coleman/Photographer's Choice), 8 (winter fox/Daniel J. Cox/The Image Bank), 9 (summer fox/Rick Price/Oxford Scientific), 10 (Beverly Joubert/National Geographic), 12 (frog fish/Reinhard Dirscherl/Waterframe), 18 (stick insect/lithops/Visuals Unlimited, Inc./Kjell Sandved), 19 (Jeff Lepore/Photographer's Choice); Naturepl.com pp.5 (yellow spider/Premaphotos), 6 (Nature Production), 11 (Jack Dykinga), 13 (David Shale), 15 (golden tortoise beetle/Doug Wechsler), 16 (leaf insect/Ian Lockwood), 17 (frog/Florian Möllers); Oxford University Press pp.8 (winter grouse); Science Photo Library p.15 (red tortoise beetle/ K Jayaram).

Introduction

What is camouflage? Animals use camouflage to hide. They use their color or their shape to hide. Sometimes you can't see the animals!

Can you see the fish?
Where is the frog?
What animal is hiding in the tree?

Now read and discover more about camouflage!

Camouflage

Animals use camouflage to hide from other animals.

This tiger is using camouflage to hide in the grass. The tiger has fur on its body. The fur has stripes. The stripes help the tiger to hide in the grass.

A Tiger

grass

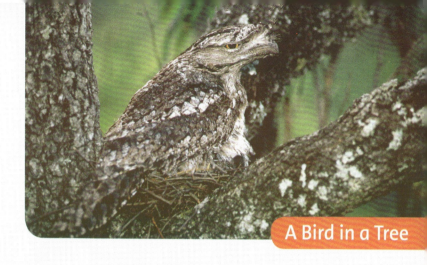

A Bird in a Tree

Some animals look the same as trees or flowers. Birds have feathers on their body. This bird has brown and white feathers. The bird is hiding in a tree. It's the same color as the tree. Can you see the bird?

Discover!

This spider hides on flowers. On yellow flowers, the spider is yellow. On white flowers, it's white!

Go to pages 20–21 for activities.

 # Animal Homes

Many animals are the same color as their home. This helps them to hide.

Let's find a caterpillar. This green caterpillar lives on a green leaf. The caterpillar is good at hiding. It looks the same as the leaf!

A Caterpillar

A Monkey

Many animals that live in trees are brown or green. Can you see this monkey? It's hiding in the trees in a rainforest.

Harp Seals

This mother harp seal is gray. She swims in the gray water. Her baby is white. The baby seal lives on the white ice. The mother and the baby are using camouflage to hide.

➡ Go to pages 22–23 for activities.

3 Winter and Summer

In winter, there's lots of snow and ice in very cold places. The animals have white fur or feathers so they can hide.

Here's an Arctic fox in winter with its white fur. Here's a grouse with its white feathers. The fox and the grouse are using camouflage.

An Arctic Fox in Winter

A Grouse in Winter

An Arctic Fox in Summer

chicks
A Grouse in Summer

In summer, the snow melts. Some animals get new fur or feathers. Their home isn't white now! See how the Arctic fox has brown fur in summer. The grouse has brown summer feathers. Her chicks have brown feathers, too.

When more snow comes in winter, the animals are white again!

→ Go to pages 24–25 for activities.

4 In the Grass

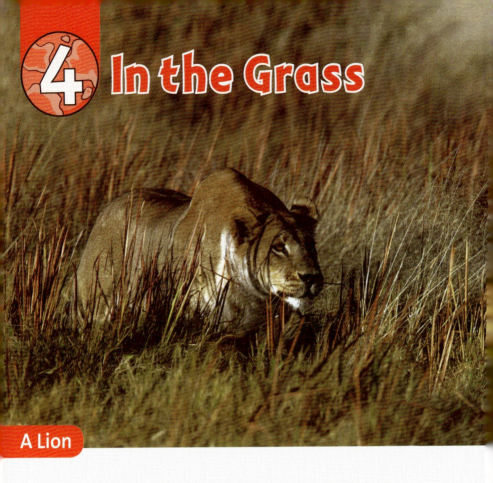

A Lion

Lots of amazing animals live in Africa. They hide in the tall grass. Some animals hunt other animals.

It's evening and here's a hungry lion. The lion wants to hunt a gazelle. The lion is hiding so gazelles can't see it. The lion is the same color as the grass.

A Gazelle

Gazelles use camouflage, too. They are the same color as the grass. Gazelles hide so lions can't see them. When a lion sees a gazelle, the gazelle runs away. Gazelles can run very fast.

A mother gazelle hides her baby in the tall grass. Lions don't see it there.

Go to pages 26–27 for activities.

5 In the Water

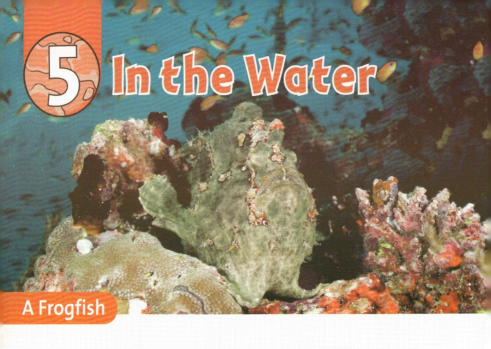

A Frogfish

Many animals use camouflage in the water. This frogfish lives next to coral. The fish looks the same as the coral. Can you see the fish?

This flounder is a fish that lives at the bottom of the ocean. It looks the same as the stones!

A Flounder

shiny scales

A Hatchet Fish

This hatchet fish lives in the deep ocean. It has very shiny scales. They look the same as a mirror. Light bounces off the scales so other animals can't see the fish.

Discover!

The leafy sea dragon looks the same as a plant. Other fish want to eat it!

Go to pages 28–29 for activities.

6 A New Color

Some animals can get a new color very fast. The cuttlefish is brown when it's on sand. When it goes on coral, it's many colors! It can make stripes and other patterns on its body, too.

A Cuttlefish

A Beetle

This beetle is shiny yellow. When a bird comes to eat the beetle, the beetle uses camouflage. The beetle gets a new color and a new pattern. Now it looks the same as a ladybug! The bird doesn't like eating ladybugs so it goes away. Then the beetle can be yellow again.

> Go to pages 30–31 for activities.

7 Is It a Leaf?

A Katydid

What's this? Is it a leaf? No, it's an insect called a katydid. It's amazing! It looks the same as a leaf.

A Leaf Insect

Here's another insect. It's called a leaf insect. When it moves, it looks the same as a leaf in the wind. The leaf insect can have holes in its body. This looks the same as a leaf when an animal eats it!

A Frog

Look at these leaves. Can you see the frog? It's using camouflage. This frog lives in a rainforest.

Can you find the animal here? It's a leaf gecko. See how it looks the same as the leaf.

A Leaf Gecko

Go to pages 32–33 for activities.

8 What Is It?

A Stick Insect

Here's a stick insect. It looks the same as a small stick. At night, it eats leaves. In the day, it hides on plants and you don't know it's there.

Lithops Plants

Are these stones? No, they are lithops plants! Animals think they are stones and they don't eat them. That's good camouflage.

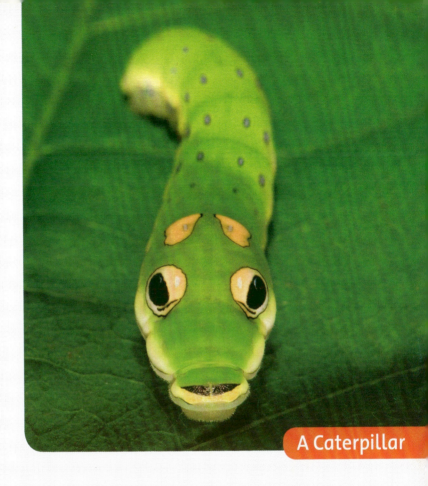

A Caterpillar

This caterpillar looks the same as a snake. It has two circles on its body. The circles look the same as a snake's eyes. When the caterpillar is scared, it makes the circles big.

Lots of animals use camouflage to hide. How many animals can you find in this book?

→ Go to pages 34–35 for activities.

1 Camouflage

← Read pages 4–5.

1 Write the words.

> spider   fur   tree   tiger   bird   flowers

1 ___fur___   2 _____   3 _____

4 _____   5 _____   6 _____

2 Find and write the words.

> (animals)camouflagehidebodycolorstripes

1 ___animals___   3 _____   5 _____
2 _____   4 _____   6 _____

20

3 Circle the correct words.

1 Animals use **spiders** / (**camouflage**) to hide.
2 **Tigers** / **Birds** have fur.
3 Birds have **flowers** / **feathers** on their body.
4 Some **tigers** / **animals** look the same as flowers.
5 Some spiders **hide** / **help** on flowers.

4 Answer the questions.

1 What do animals use to hide?
   <u>Animals use camouflage to hide.</u>
2 What do tigers have on their body?
   _____
3 How do stripes help tigers?
   _____
4 What do birds have on their body?
   _____
5 Where do some spiders hide?
   _____

2 Animal Homes

← Read pages 6–7.

1 Complete the puzzle.

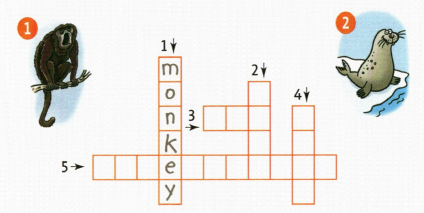

2 Write *true* or *false*.

1 Caterpillars live on leaves.   true
2 Harp seals live in rainforests.   ____
3 Baby harp seals are white.   ____
4 Monkeys live on ice.   ____

3 Complete the sentences.

brown   ice   hiding   ~~color~~   swim   rainforests

1 Many animals are the same ___color___ as their home.
2 Caterpillars are good at _____.
3 Many animals that live in trees are _____.
4 Monkeys hide in _____.
5 Mother harp seals _____.
6 Baby harp seals live on _____.

4 Order the words.

1 gray. / mother / is / The / harp seal
   ___The mother harp seal is gray.___
2 harp seal / swims / The / mother / in / the / water.
   _____
3 white. / is / harp seal / baby / The
   _____
4 harp seal / on / baby / lives / The / ice.
   _____

3 Winter and Summer

← Read pages 8–9.

1 Write the words.

1 xfo   2 sheaterf   3 reumms

fox

4 trewin   5 sorgue   6 ruf

2 What color are they? Match.

1 brown — Arctic fox in winter
2 white — grouse in summer
3 white — Arctic fox in summer
4 brown — grouse in winter

3 Complete the sentences.

> melts   white   feathers
> summer   snow   brown

1 The Arctic fox has brown fur in _____ .
2 The grouse has white _____ in winter.
3 The grouse has _____ feathers in summer.
4 The Arctic fox has _____ fur in winter.
5 There's lots of _____ in winter.
6 In summer, the snow _____ .

4 Answer the questions.

1 How do animals hide in snow?
   _____
2 What color is the grouse in summer?
   _____
3 What color is the Arctic fox in winter?
   _____
4 When does the snow melt?
   _____

4 In the Grass

← Read pages 10–11.

1 Find and write the words.

h	t	i	h	d	e
g	a	z	e	l	l
l	i	h	u	n	t
b	g	r	a	s	s
a	r	l	i	o	n

1 hide   2 h_____

3 l_____   4 g_____   5 g_____

2 Write *true* or *false*.

1 Lots of amazing animals live in Africa. _____
2 Animals in Africa hide in the snow. _____
3 Some animals hunt other animals. _____
4 Gazelles hunt lions. _____
5 Lions run away from gazelles. _____
6 Gazelles use camouflage. _____

3 Match. Then write the sentences.

Lots of animals	so gazelles can't see it.
Some animals hide in	very fast.
A lion hides	so lions can't see it.
A gazelle hides	the grass.
Gazelles can run	live in Africa.

1 Lots of animals live in Africa.
2 _____
3 _____
4 _____
5 _____

4 Circle the correct words.

1 Animals hide in the **grass** / **gazelle**.
2 Some animals **run** / **hunt** other animals.
3 Gazelles **use** / **hide** camouflage.
4 **Lions** / **Gazelles** run away.
5 A gazelle hides its **baby** / **mother**.

5 In the Water

← Read pages 12–13.

1 Write the words.

> ocean   coral   mirror   fish   stones   scales

1 _____   2 _____   3 _____

4 _____   5 _____   6 _____

2 Where do they live? Match.

1 frogfish
2 flounder
3 hatchet fish
4 leafy sea dragon

next to plants
in the deep ocean
next to coral
at the bottom of the ocean

3 Order the words.

1 next to / The / frogfish / lives / coral.

_____

2 looks / The / flounder / stones. / as / the / the same

_____

3 scales. / shiny / has / The / hatchet fish

_____

4 The / looks / leafy sea dragon / the same plant. / as a

_____

4 Answer the questions.

1 How does the frogfish use camouflage?

_____

2 Where does the flounder live?

_____

3 Where does the hatchet fish live?

_____

4 How does the leafy sea dragon use camouflage?

_____

6 A New Color

← Read pages 14–15.

1 Complete the puzzle.

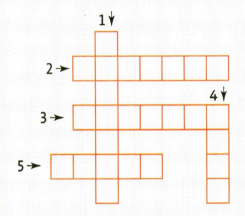

2 Write *true* or *false*.

1 The cuttlefish is brown when it's on coral. _____

2 The cuttlefish can make stripes on its body. _____

3 The beetle uses camouflage. _____

4 The beetle looks the same as a cuttlefish. _____

5 The bird likes eating ladybugs. _____

3 Number the sentences in order.

- ☐ The beetle gets a new color and a new pattern.
- ☐ The bird goes away.
- ☐ 1 The beetle is yellow.
- ☐ The beetle is yellow again.
- ☐ The beetle looks the same as a ladybug.
- ☐ A bird comes to eat the beetle.

4 Complete the sentences.

> pattern   ladybugs   camouflage
> beetle   body   brown

1 The cuttlefish is _____ when it's on sand.

2 The cuttlefish can make patterns on its _____.

3 The beetle uses _____. It gets a new color and a new _____.

4 The _____ looks the same as a ladybug.

5 The bird doesn't like eating _____.

7 Is It a Leaf?

← Read pages 16–17.

1 Write the words.

| leaf   hole   gecko   rainforest   frog   insects |

1 _____   2 _____   3 _____

4 _____   5 _____   6 _____

2 Circle the correct words.

1 The katydid is **a frog** / **an insect**.
2 The leaf insect has **holes** / **leaves** in its body.
3 The frog lives in a **gecko** / **rainforest**.
4 The gecko looks the same as a **leaf** / **frog**.

3 Order the words.

1 the same / looks / leaf. / as a / The / katydid
   _____

2 in its / leaf insect / The / body. / has holes
   _____

3 lives / rainforest. / The / frog / in a
   _____

4 leaf gecko / The / camouflage. / uses
   _____

4 Complete the sentences.

> camouflage   gecko   leaf
> holes   animals   wind

1 Some _____ look the same as a leaf.
2 The katydid looks the same as a _____ .
3 When the leaf insect moves, it looks the same as a leaf in the _____ .
4 The leaf insect can have _____ in its body.
5 The frog uses _____ .
6 The _____ looks the same as a leaf.

8 What Is It?

← Read pages 18–19.

1 Match. Then write the sentences.

Stick insects
Lithops plants
Some caterpillars
Lots of animals use

look the same as a snake.
camouflage to hide.
look the same as a stick.
look the same as stones.

1 _____
2 _____
3 _____
4 _____

2 Find and write the words.

insectsplantsstonesanimalscaterpillarsnake

1 _____   3 _____   5 _____
2 _____   4 _____   6 _____

3 Answer the questions.

1 What does the caterpillar look the same as?
_____

2 What does the caterpillar have on its body?
_____

3 What does the caterpillar do when it's scared?
_____

4 Complete the puzzle. Then find the secret word.

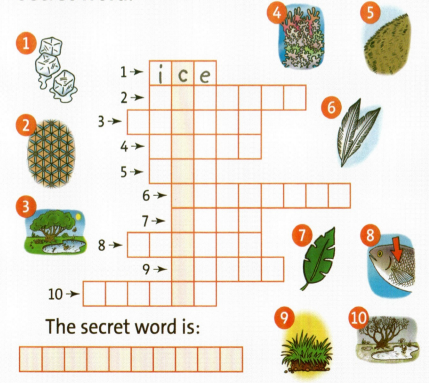

1 → i c e

The secret word is:

Project 1 — A Camouflage Poster

1 Think of an animal that uses camouflage. Complete the diagram.

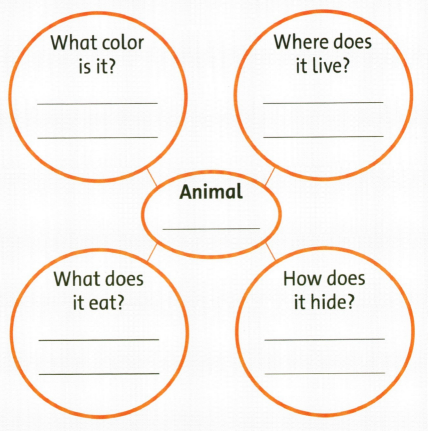

2 Find or draw pictures of the animal. Make a poster.

3 Display your poster.

Project 2 Camouflage Cards

1 Write a card about a small animal.

Animal	caterpillar
Color	green
Home	leaf
Camouflage	It's the same color as its home.

Animal	
Color	
Home	
Camouflage	

2 Write a card about a big animal.

Animal	
Color	
Home	
Camouflage	

Picture Dictionary

 bottom
 caterpillar
 coral
 deep

 fast
 feathers
 fur
 grass

 hide
 hole
 hunt
 ice

 insects
 ladybug
 leaf
 light

 melt	 mirror	 ocean	pattern
 plants	 rainforest	same	 sand
 scales	 seal	 shapes	 snake
spider	 stick	 stones	 stripes

Oxford Read and Discover

Series Editor: Hazel Geatches • CLIL Adviser: John Clegg

Oxford Read and Discover graded readers are at six levels, for students from age 6 and older. They cover many topics within three subject areas, and support English across the curriculum, or Content and Language Integrated Learning (CLIL).

Available for each reader:
- Audio Pack
- Activity Book

Available for selected readers:
- e-Books

Teaching notes & CLIL guidance: www.oup.com/elt/teacher/readanddiscover

Subject Area / Level	The World of Science & Technology	The Natural World	The World of Arts & Social Studies
1 — 300 headwords	• Eyes • Fruit • Trees • Wheels	• At the Beach • In the Sky • Wild Cats • Young Animals	• Art • Schools
2 — 450 headwords	• Electricity • Plastic • Sunny and Rainy • Your Body	• Camouflage • Earth • Farms • In the Mountains	• Cities • Jobs
3 — 600 headwords	• How We Make Products • Sound and Music • Super Structures • Your Five Senses	• Amazing Minibeasts • Animals in the Air • Life in Rainforests • Wonderful Water	• Festivals Around the World • Free Time Around the World
4 — 750 headwords	• All About Plants • How to Stay Healthy • Machines Then and Now • Why We Recycle	• All About Desert Life • All About Ocean Life • Animals at Night • Incredible Earth	• Animals in Art • Wonders of the Past
5 — 900 headwords	• Materials to Products • Medicine Then and Now • Transportation Then and Now • Wild Weather	• All About Islands • Animal Life Cycles • Exploring Our World • Great Migrations	• Homes Around the World • Our World in Art
6 — 1,050 headwords	• Cells and Microbes • Clothes Then and Now • Incredible Energy • Your Amazing Body	• All About Space • Caring for Our Planet • Earth Then and Now • Wonderful Ecosystems	• Food Around the World • Helping Around the World